# Pan-Islamism

Chirol, Valentine, Sir

BIBLIOLIFE

Copyright © BiblioLife, LLC

This historical reproduction is part of a unique project that provides opportunities for readers, educators and researchers by bringing hard-to-find original publications back into print at reasonable prices. Because this and other works are culturally important, we have made them available as part of our commitment to protecting, preserving and promoting the world's literature. These books are in the "public domain" and were digitized and made available in cooperation with libraries, archives, and open source initiatives around the world dedicated to this important mission.

We believe that when we undertake the difficult task of re-creating these works as attractive, readable and affordable books, we further the goal of sharing these works with a global audience, and preserving a vanishing wealth of human knowledge.

Many historical books were originally published in small fonts, which can make them very difficult to read. Accordingly, in order to improve the reading experience of these books, we have created "enlarged print" versions of our books. Because of font size variation in the original books, some of these may not technically qualify as "large print" books, as that term is generally defined; however, we believe these versions provide an overall improved reading experience for many.

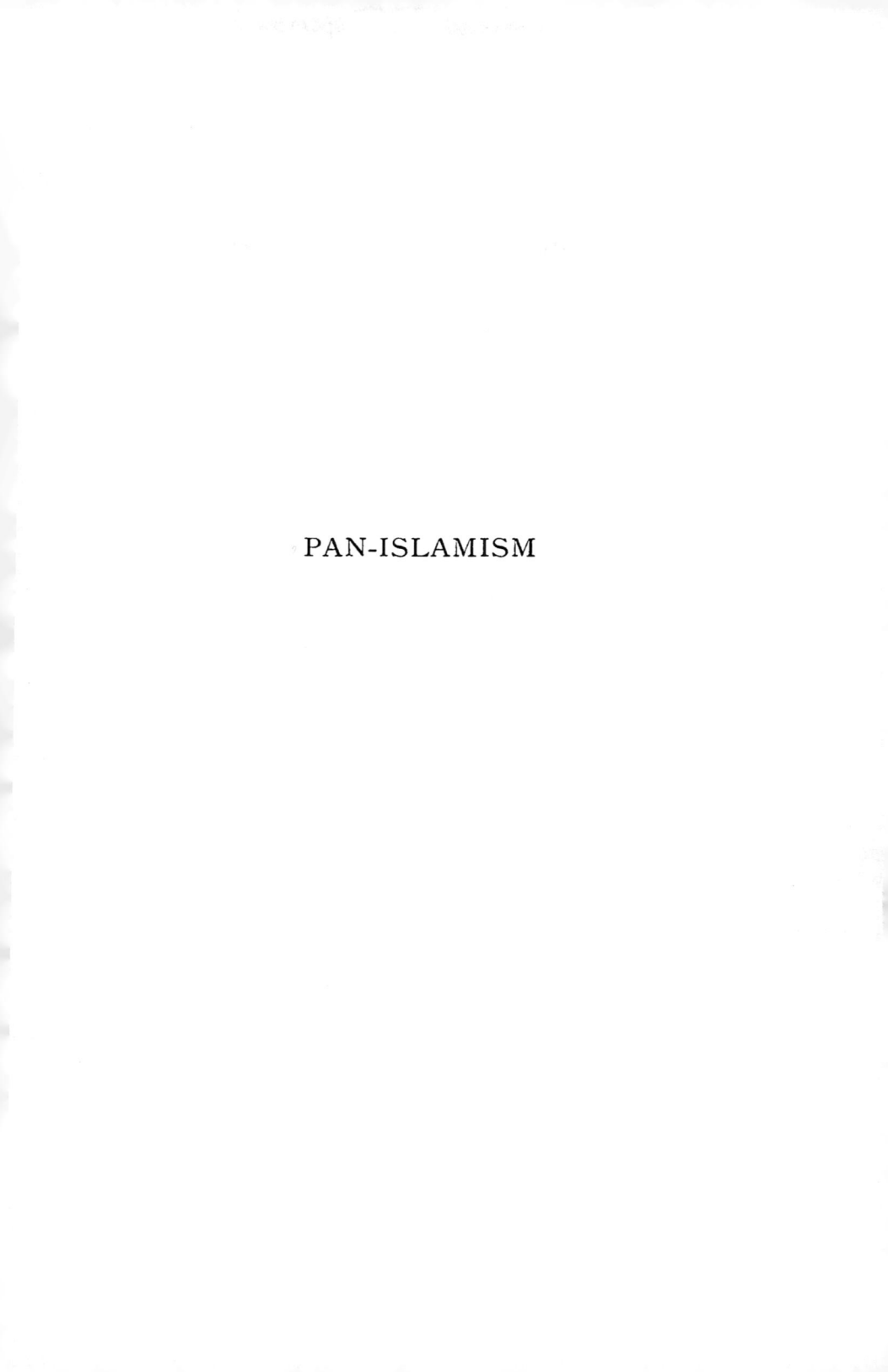

# PAN-ISLAMISM

# PAN-ISLAMISM

WE often speak—rather light-heartedly—of the British Empire as, amongst other things, the greatest Mahomedan power in the world, and unquestionably no sovereign counts amongst his subjects so many millions of Mahomedans as King Edward. The total number of Mahomedans in the world is approximately estimated at some 250,000,000. Of these barely one-tenth own direct allegiance to the Sultan of Turkey, whereas there are no less than sixty-two millions within the frontiers of our Indian Empire, and millions more are to be found scattered about our possessions and protectorates in Malaya, and in Eastern, Central, and Western Africa, whilst in Egypt and the Sudan we have assumed responsibility for another twelve million followers of the Prophet. This is unquestionably a factor of the very greatest importance in considering the interests and the future of the British Empire, for in the East religion is still a force more potent than any other; and in this, as in many other respects, the East stands much where Europe stood in the Middle Ages. Both in Egypt and in India we have recently had reminders—which have come as a surprise to many of us —that Islam especially still represents an elemental force with which British statesmanship may have seriously to reckon. From this point of view I thought it might be of some interest to collect a few notes concerning the history and growth of the movement which is now known as Pan-Islamism, in connection more particularly with its influence upon India.

It is just thirty years since the present Sulan Abdul Hamid came to the throne of Turkey. His Empire then seemed to be on the point of dissolution. His treasury was bankrupt. His Christian provinces were in revolt. Within two years a victorious Russian army was encamped at the gates of his capital. He himself was deemed to be a mere puppet in the hands of the powerful bureaucratic oligarchy which, after a succession of Palace conspiracies, had placed him upon the throne. We may reprobate the ruthlessness of his methods, but we cannot refuse our admiration to the consummate ability, the resourcefulness and the inflexibility of purpose with which Abdul Hamid —certainly one of the most striking figures of our times—faced so desperate a situation, and applied himself with mingled daring and cunning to the two-fold task of restoring the despotic power of the Sultanate at home, and of seeking compensation for the curtailment of his temporal dominions by reviving and extending throughout the Mahomedan world the spiritual authority to which he lays claim as heir to the Khalifate of Islam. With regard to his domestic policy, all I need say is that, however severely we may condemn it according to our own standards, it has been from his point of view eminently successful. The old oligarchy, which under his predecessors ruled Turkey from the Sublime Porte, has been swept away, and though Abdul Hamid never issues forth from his wellguarded Palace of Yeldiz Kiosk, the Sultan's will is the only law which to-day governs the Turkish Empire unto its uttermost limits. What I propose to deal with this afternoon is the influence which Abdul Hamid exercises, and projects far beyond the immediate frontiers of the Turkish Empire, as the Khalif whose spiritual supremacy is proclaimed every week in the *Khutbeh*, or Friday prayer, which is read in all the mosques of Sunni Mahomedans within his dominions, and in many mosques beyond them. This prayer runs as follows :

O ALLAH, Mercifully help the "Just Khalifs" (*i.e.*, Abu-Bekr, Omar, Osman and Ali) and the IMAMS MEHDI (*i e.*, the descendants of Ali) who have administered justly and equitably. O Allah, strengthen and assist Thy Slave and Khalif, the Most powerful Sultan, the Most Glorious Khan, the Shadow of ALLAH on Earth, the Lord of the Kings of the Arabs and the Ajems, the Servant of the Twain Holy Places, the Sultan and Son of a Sultan, SULTAN el GHAZI, ABDUL HAMID KHAN, Son of the Sultan el GHAZI ABDUL MEJID KHAN, Son of the Sultan el GHAZI MAHMOUD KHAN.

May ALLAH preserve his Khalifate and strengthen with Justice his Sultanate, and may His benefits and favours be showered upon the whole world up to the end of All Times. AMEN.

In theory it is easy enough to dispute the claims of the Turkish Sultans to the Khalifate. The title of Khalif, it will be remembered, was that assumed by the immediate successors of Mahomed as vicegerents of the Prophet. In the earliest days of Islam the succession of the Khalifate give rise to the first great Mahomedan schism—a schism which has been perpetuated to the present day, between Sunnis and Shiahs, Persia being now the one important Mussulman power that represents the latter sect. It was undoubtedly held by the early doctors of Mussulman law that the Khalif himself must belong to the Arab tribe of El Koreish, and that he must be elected by the suffrages of the whole Mussulman community. But the process of election soon became a mere formality, and practically fell into desuetude long before the Khalifate had passed out of Arab hands. It became merely an honorific title, which was indeed at one time borne simultaneously by the independent rulers of different portions of the Mussulman world in Baghdad, Cairo, and Cordova.

The claim of the Turkish Sultans to the Khalifate dates only from the sixteenth century, and arises out of the conquest of Egypt, where the fugitive descendants of the Abasside Khalifs who had formerly reigned in Baghdad were allowed to retain a shadowy authority, which lent to the turbulent Mameluke rulers of Cairo a certain spiritual prestige. The story is worth recalling, for the spirit in which Selim I. compassed the conquest of Egypt would seem to have inspired in no small measure the latest of his successors on the Ottoman throne. The authority of the Egyptian Mamelukes extended, at the beginning of the sixteenth century, over the whole of Syria and Arabia to the valley of the Euphrates. But in 1512 there came to the throne of Turkey, in the person of Selim I., a Sultan who combined with the devouring ambition of his ancestors a novel tendency towards philosophic mysticism, and a curious craving for spiritual illumination. Poet, philosopher, and theologian, as well as conqueror, he was the first Ottoman Sultan to conceive the idea that the most powerful of Mohamedan princes might well claim to be also the paramount prince of Islam and the vicegerent of the Prophet. The first war waged by him was in the nature of a religious war. It was waged against Shah Ismail of Persia; it began with a wholesale massacre of Shiahs throughout Selim's dominions, and it ended with the complete overthrow of the Persian army at Tchaldiran, not to the wonted Turkish war-cry of " Padishah, Padishah," but to the essentially Mahomedan war-cry of " Allah, Allah." Selim's armies continued their career of conquest through Kurdistan into Mesopotamia, and thus ultimately came into direct collision with the forces of the Egyptian Mameluke Sultans in the Euphrates valley. Selim himself had by that time returned to Adrianople, and the various incidents related by Turkish historians throw an interesting light upon the frame of mind which determined his expedition to Egypt. The possession of the holy places of Arabia had already fired Selim's imagination, and all his courtiers harped upon this theme. His Vizier, Ahmed Pasha, who was all for war, taunted Selim with the story of how in his youth he had been a prisoner in Cairo in the hands of Kait Bey, and how the latter had boasted that the power of Egypt would always close the road to Mecca and Medina against the Turkish hordes. Selim's chief secretary impressed upon him that in Cairo, both actually and metaphorically, must be sought the keys of the Holy Places. His Master of the Ceremonies dreamt opportunely that the four disciples of the Prophet appeared to him waving victorious standards. This supernatural lead Selim was bound to follow, and he set forth in person to take command of the expedition in June 1516. The octogenarian Mameluke Sultan of Egypt, Kans Ghaury, had in the meantime collected the flower of his forces near Aleppo, at Merjdabik, near the reputed tomb of David. His defeat was as complete as had been Shah Ismail's, and Selim held a triumphal entry into Aleppo, where for the first time at the Friday service in the Mosque, the title of Protector of the Holy Places was added to the other titles of the Ottoman Sultan. Such was Selim's delight that, following the example of the Prophet, who bestowed his own coat on Kaab Ibn Soheir for a poem of homage and good tidings, the Sultan took off the costly robe he was wearing and placed it on the shoulders of the officiating divine. At Damascus, where Selim paused for some weeks in his victorious progress towards Egypt, he spent, we are told, most of his time within the precincts of the wonderful Mosque of St. John, discoursing with learned doctors of Mohamedan law, and from the greatest of them, Sheikh Mohamed of Bedakshan, who had preached before him on the duties and responsibilities of the Kalifate, he implored and received a solemn blessing on his undertakings. Marching southward along the coast, Selim turned aside for a few days to make a pious pilgrimage to Jerusalem, which is still, next to Mecca and Medina, the holiest city in the eyes of the Mahomedans. He reached Cairo early in 1517. The Mameluke Sultans of Egypt and their followers were destroyed root and branch, but the last scion of the Abbasside Khalifs, El Muttawwakil, was not only spared but treated with the utmost show of deference. Having formally transferred to Selim the somewhat shadowy title he himself possessed to the Vicegerency of the Prophet, he was carried back with the conqueror to Constantinople, and together with him what was, perhaps, still more valuable, the famous *Bordah* or mantle of the Prophet, which had been for centuries the most cherished heirloom of the Abbassides. Whether, according to Mohamedan law, Muttawwakil was competent to convey to Selim a good title to the Kalifate is no doubt a moot point, but possession is nine points of the law in the East as in the West, perhaps even more so in the East. In Cairo, as had been foretold to him, Selim received from Mohamed Abdul Barakat, the thirty-fourth Grand Sherif of Mecca, through the hands of his son and special envoy, the keys of the sacred Kaaba, the immemorial shrine of

Islam, and the title already conferred upon him at Aleppo, of Servant of the Holy Places, thus received practical confirmation. Before leaving Cairo Selim took care to discharge his new responsibilities by making elaborate provisions for the despatch, under his auspices, of the annual pilgrims' caravan to Mecca, which had been hitherto one of the privileges of the rulers of Egypt, and the presents which accompanied it for the people of Mecca and Medina were on a scale of lavish munificence well calculated to secure their loyalty.

From that day to this none of Selim's successors has allowed the title to lapse. In the heyday of their military power, it is true, the Sultans were content to rely upon the keenness of their scimitar rather than upon spiritual power. The first Sultan who attempted to make capital out of his authority as Khalif in support of his temporal policy seems to have been Mustapha III., and it is interesting to note that this new departure coincides almost exactly with the first attempt of a great European Power to interfere in the internal affairs of Turkey as the champion of the Christian subject races. Catherine II. had sent Admiral Orloff into the Mediterranean during the recent war with Turkey in order to induce the Greek populations of the Morea and Magnesia to rise against their oppressors. During the peace negotiations at Fokshani in 1772, one of the conditions demanded by Russia was the recognition by Turkey of the independence of the Crimean Tartars. To this demand Sultan Mustapha replied by a *non possumus* based upon his duties as Khalif. He declared formally that to him as Khalif belonged spiritual supremacy over all Sunni Mussulmans, and that if he did not fully exercise that supremacy over India, Bokhara, Morocco, and other countries whose rulers were Sunni Mussulmans, this was due merely to material difficulties of distance, but that he would be neglecting his duties as Khalif if he agreed to surrender the Tartars to the dominion of a Christian Power. This interesting claim proved, however, of little avail against Catherine's big battalions, and the Treaty of Kutchuk-Kainaidji, on the contrary, introduced a new principle of which the subsequent application in a far more extended form has repeatedly affected and still largely governs the relations between Turkey and the rest of Europe, for it recognised the right of the Russian Ambassador at Constantinople to intervene with the Porte on behalf of the Sultan's Christian subjects in the Danubian provinces.

Perhaps because Mustapha's appeal to his authority as Khalif failed so lamentably on that occasion, the Khalifate dropped into the background, as far as Europe was concerned, for another century. Indeed, after the Crimean War and the

Treaty of Paris, when Turkey was admitted into the comity of European nations, her chief anxiety was, at least as far as outward forms were concerned, to merge the Oriental in the Occidental, and in international documents we find even the title of Sultan transmuted into the westernised designation of Emperor of the Ottomans. Abdul Hamid, however, is a keen student of the history of his own country, and it may well be Mustapha's claim which first inspired him to revive for his own benefit the pretensions of his less successful ancestor. Certain it is that for the last five and twenty years his policy both within and without his immediate dominions has been more and more closely bound up with his claim to the spiritual headship of Islam. Although it was to British intervention that Abdul Hamid mainly owed the mitigation of the harsh terms of peace imposed upon him by Russia in the Treaty of Saint Stephano, the relations of friendliness between this country and Turkey which followed the Berlin Congress were not of long duration. With the advent of Mr. Gladstone's administration in 1880 Great Britain assumed the lead in a policy of suasion and even of coercion, which though not in itself by any means antagonistic to the real interests of Turkey, frequently wore an outward aspect of hostility to the Sultan and to his Mahomedan subjects in the exclusive interests of his Christian subjects. In the eyes of Mahomedans, at least, the action of the European Concert, headed by England, often assumed the aspect of a religious crusade directed against the ascendency of the ruling Moslem race in Turkey. It is not unnatural that in these circumstances the Sultan should have been led to conceive a counter policy by which the forces of Islam should be brought together and organised for the purpose of resistance to the pressure of Christendom. Equally excusable was it that as to England had fallen the lead in bringing the pressure of Christendom to bear upon Turkey, the Sultan should have seen in a Mussulman revival possibilities of effective reprisals against that European Power which of all others had the largest Mahomedan element to reckon with in its own dominions.

It was during the complications which led to the British occupation of Egypt that Yeldish Kiosk appears to have become the seat of an organised propaganda on behalf of what has come to be known as Pan-Islamism. That was five and twenty years ago, and the channels through which Pan-Islamism works are so tortuous, its ramifications so subtle, that its slow and steady progress attracted but little attention except from those who know something of the East, and who were generally jeered at for their pains as visionaries and alarmists—until the events of the last twelve months in Egypt revealed as in a sudden blaze of light the activity of forces which we had ignored with our usual self-complacency because they are difficult to reconcile with our own conception of the fitness of things. Whilst Europe had been vainly protesting and demonstrating against Armenian and Macedonian atrocities, and European diplomacy at Constantinople had been reduced to impotency by its own intestinal jealousies, emissaries had been constantly passing to and fro between Yeldiz Kiosk and Mahomedan centres throughout the Eastern world, spreading the fame of the ever-victorious Khalif, who had drowned rebellion at home in rivers of infidel blood and stubbornly defied the wrath of the Powers. Had not the mightiest of all the potentates of Christendom, the great War Lord of Germany, humbly travelled to Constantinople to do homage to the Padishah, and openly proclaimed himself at Damascus, "the devoted friend of the 300,000,000 Mussulmans who own His Majesty the Sultan Abdul Hamid to be their Khalif?" Surely the sword of Islam had sprung once more from the scabbard in which it had too long rusted. The word prestige is deprecated nowadays in humanitarian quarters as redolent of obsolete militarism and alien barbarism; but in the East it has lost none of its potency, and throughout the East, wherever Mahomedans congregate, in the porches of Mosques, in the bazaars of crowded cities, in wild mountain fastnesses, in the tents of the wandering nomads, in the great religious fairs, and above all, at that world-centre of Mussulman pilgrimage under the shadow of the Kaabah of Mecca, the name of Abdul Hamid has been sedulously magnified for the last quarter of a century with the results which we are now for the first time beginning to realise.

Amongst the concrete facts which demonstrate the earnestness and thoroughness of Abdul Hamid's Pan-Islamic policy, none is more remarkable and significant than the construction of the Hejaz Railway, which will ultimately link up the seat of his temporal power as Sultan at Constantinople with the seat of his spiritual power as Khalif at Mecca. A very full and valuable description of this railway was contributed in August last to *Petermann's Mittheilungen*, the well-known German magazine of geography and exploration, by General Auler Pasha, a Prussian officer of Engineers in the service of the Sultan. The following details are borrowed from it. The railway, which starts from Damascus and follows in the main the old pilgrim road to Mecca, was begun in 1901, and before the end of the year reached Deráa, whence a branch line of about 100 miles now connects with Haiffa on the Mediterranean. In 1904 it reached Ma'an, which was used as a military base for the despatch of troops to Akabah and Tabah during the Turco-

Egyptian controversy last spring. It has now reached Tebuk, which is half-way between Damascus and Medina, and next year it will reach Medain-Salih, a very important strategic point in connection with Nejd and Central Arabia. The total length of the line from Damascus to Mecca will be about 1100 miles, of which 435 miles have been opened to traffic. The rate of construction, which is increasing, now averages about 100 miles a year, and the railway is expected to reach Medina in 1910, and Mecca about three years later. The cost is estimated at a little more than £3000 a mile, or altogether perhaps four millions sterling, including the branch from Deráa to Haiffa, and the prolongation from Mecca to Jeddah on the Red Sea—an extraordinarily small sum, considering the engineering difficulties and the still greater difficulties of transport and supply in a region which is almost entirely desert and waterless. The explanation is that no financial provision has to be made either for the acquisition of land or for the payment of labour. The land is the Sultan's, and the labour is supplied by the troops. Three battalions of infantry, each 1000 strong; two railway battalions, each 1200 strong; one company of Pioneers, and a detachment of the Telegraph Service Corps have been furnished by the Fifth Army Corps from Damascus, and recently two more infantry battalions from the Sixth Army Corps have been ordered up from Baghdad. A German engineer-in-chief, Meissner Pasha, with about a dozen German, Austrian and Swiss engineers, is in charge of the railway works, under the supreme direction of Field-Marshal Kiazim Pasha.

To General Auler's technical report, General von der Goltz, the very distinguished officer of the German General Staff who for so many years presided over the reorganisation of the Turkish army, has written a most instructive preface, of which the following is a summary :

> The world at large hardly heard of the Hejaz Railway until on September 1, 1904, H.M. the Sultan Abdul Hamid, on the anniversary of his accession to the throne, caused the opening of the line as far as the little town of Maan, in a remote southern corner of Syria, to be celebrated with a pomp and ceremony of which the echo resounded throughout the Mahomedan world. . . . To-day a considerable portion of the line is already completed, and the work of construction is being pushed on with an energy which shows not only what Turkey is capable of doing when the Sultan has proclaimed his will, but also how powerful is the religious sentiment of Islam. Contributions to the Hejaz Railway constitute a deed of piety, and that word has lost none of its magic in the East.
>
> The railway, covering a distance of about 1100 miles, follows for the most part the old caravan route over which thousands and thousands of pious Mussulmans have braved the tedium and dangers of the long journey in order to accompany the yearly offerings of the Sultan to the Holy Places. This journey

will ultimately take only five days, and vast numbers of his subjects from
Europe and from Asia Minor will be able, as never before, to achieve their
hearts' desire and perform their devotions on the spot where the Prophet himself lived and died. To the elder generation this must sound as a fairy tale,
and the Sultan could hardly have conceived an undertaking better calculated
to enhance his prestige amongst all the peoples of Islam. By the time the
railway reaches the gates of Mecca, it will undoubtedly be linked up from
Damascus, *viâ* Aleppo, with the Anatolian system and the Baghdad line, and
there will thus be an unbroken iron road from Constantinople to the Sacred
City.

Abdul Hamid's rule is inspired with the steady unswerving purpose of
bringing into closer and mightier cohesion the whole Mahomedan world under
his sceptre, or, at least, under his influence. Of late years his efforts have
been directed specially to Arabia, where the acknowledgment of Turkish
supremacy has made great strides, though in the land of Yemen, the ancient
Arabia Felix, the struggle has yet to be fiercely fought out. The policy of the
Sultan, directed to what may be called internal conquests, which shall com-
pensate him in the Islamic world for the losses suffered on the fringe of his
Empire under the pressure of Christendom, will receive a mighty impulse from
the opening of the railway to the Holy Places. The remoteness of the southern
provinces of his dominions has been a serious cause of military weakness in
the past. But all this will be altered when railways reach from Constantinople
to the Red Sea and the Persian Gulf. Turkey will then regain, as it were, a
new lease of youth and vigour.

So far General von der Goltz. There are other aspects of
the policy embodied in the Hejaz Railway upon which he
does not dwell though they are clearly present to his mind.
At present the Sultan's position in Arabia, much as he has
already done to consolidate it, depends very largely upon
British good-will. The vast majority of the forces which he
has poured into Arabia, and especially into the Yemen, where
a ten years' campaign has not yet broken the stubborn resistance of the tribes, have been transported by sea. Men
as well as supplies and warlike stores of every description
have to be sent across the Mediterranean through the Suez
Canal and down the Red Sea. What that means with our
command of the sea and our dominant position in Egypt, I
need not point out. The completion of the Hejaz Railway
will in a large measure relieve the Sultan from the galling
dependence upon friendly relations with Great Britain which
the maintenance of his main line of communications with
Arabia now necessitates.

It is not, however, only as a means of securing continuous
land communication between Constantinople and the Holy
Places that the construction of the Hejaz Railway will
strengthen the strategic position of Turkey in Arabia. The
existence of practically independent principalities in Central
Arabia such as that which Ibn-el-Rashid carved out for himself

in Nejd, has from time to time been a severe thorn in the flesh to the Sultans. Next year, as we have already seen, the Hejaz Railway will reach Medain Salih, and as that place is about the best jumping-ground for Nejd *via* Teyna, the arrival of railhead there must vastly strengthen the Turkish position throughout Central and South-Eastern Arabia, right down to the Persian Gulf. We have only to remember the large share which our own *protégé*, the Sheikh of Koweyt, has played during the last few years in the struggle for power between the descendants of the old Wahibi Emirs and the successors of Muhammed Ibn-el-Rashid, in order to realise how severely the establishment of Turkish supremacy in the Gebel Shammar might press upon our allies along the Arabian shores of the Persian Gulf. I had an opportunity of discussing this question a few years ago with the Sheikh of Koweyt himself, whose friendly relations with the Indian Government had given deep umbrage to Turkey. In fact Turkish troops had moved out from Bassorah and Baghdad, and the presence of British ships had alone averted the aggressive intervention of the Turks. Nevertheless, Sheikh Mubarak professed to entertain little apprehension with regard to Turkish aggression from that quarter, but laid great stress upon the necessity for him of keeping his communications open with Arabia, and of securing the independence of Nejd from Turkish control by retaining it in possession of his Wahabi friends.

Nor is it only in connection with our own position in the Persian Gulf that the consolidation of Turkish power in the Arabian Peninsula may directly affect British interests. The history of India within relatively recent times offers a very striking example of the influence which events in Arabia can exercise upon the Mahomedan population of India. One of the most important religious movements amongst Indian Mahomedans under British rule was the direct result of the great Mahomedan revival in Arabia towards the end of the eighteenth and the beginning of the nineteenth century, known as Wahabism, after its founder, Mohammed Wahab, of Nejd, That movement, it will be remembered, swept over the whole of Arabia, and for a time wrested even the Holy Places from the power of the Sultans, who had to call in the aid of Mehemet Ali, the great Pasha of Egypt, to stamp it out by sheer force. One of Wahab's disciples, Seyyid Ahmad Shah of Bareilly, introduced his doctrines into India in 1826, and preached a holy war against the Sikh confederacy, which was then supreme in the Northern Punjab. Notwithstanding the enthusiasm with which his teachings were welcomed, the movement in that part of India proved abortive, but some of its adherents established themselves permanently both In the North-West and in the Western districts of Bengal, where they made their headquarters at Patna. From the latter place, especially, they sent out emissaries all over India, and notably into Eastern Bengal, where Hajji Sharnet Ullah, who had himself been at Mecca and come into personal contact with Wahab, became an active missionary of the new doctrine. He made a large number of converts, especially amongst the lower classes, and both he and his son after him, waged successful war against the Hindu superstitions which had continued to maintain their hold over the followers of the Prophet. Their proceedings were often lawless and brought them frequently into conflict with the British authorities. But they undoubtedly gave a powerful impetus to Mahomedan feeling throughout Eastern Bengal, and also in Behar.

Before proceeding, however, to the consideration of the effect which the growth of Abdul Hamid's prestige as a leader of Islam has produced upon the Mahomedans of India, I want to draw your attention to a very significant movement which has been going on in Persia, the one country where the Shiah form of Islam is supreme. One would have imagined that the bitter hatred which has subsisted for thirteen centuries between Shiahs and Sunnis would have rendered Persia inaccessible to the Pan-Islamic propaganda of a Sunni Sultan, though the possession by Turkey of the Holy Places of Arabia, to which the duty of pilgrimage is imposed on both Shiahs and Sunnis, and also of the shrines more peculiarly sacred to the Shiahs— such as Kerbela and Meshed Ali, in the valley of the Euphrates —necessarily confers upon the Sultans a prestige which the Persians are compelled to recognise, and in various treaties concluded between Sultan and Shah, the former's title of "Protector of the Holy Places" is duly recognised. But the danger to which the independence of Persia, like that of Turkey, has been exposed by the growing pressure of the Western Powers has unquestionably been used with no little effect of recent years by the missionaries of the Sultan to bring home to the people of Persia the expediency of sinking sectarian differences in the common cause of Islam. The unpopularity of the present Shah amongst the clergy of Persia, who have openly charged him with selling his country to the infidel, is so great that on several occasions the protests against his misgovernment have taken the form of threats to appeal to the protection of the Sultan, even if such protection were to involve a reconciliation with Sunnism. About two years ago the

Mujtehids, or High Priests, of Kerbela were stated to have openly threatened the Shah with excommunication for his subserviency to an infidel power, and even these high ecclesiastics, whose fortunes would seem to be indissolubly bound up with Shiism, did not hesitate to hint that the time was at hand when Shiahs as well as Sunnis would be compelled to take refuge under the sheltering ægis of the one great Mahomedan Sovereign who had proved himself to be the providential protector of Islam.

It would be still more interesting to have some really trustworthy data respecting the presence of Pan-Islamic influences in Afghanistan, the only survivor to-day, but a survivor full of vitality, of the independent Mahomedan States of Central Asia. But so rigidly is Afghanistan closed against foreign intercourse, in spite of our Treaty relations with the Ameer, that our information in regard to the present condition of affairs is altogether scanty, and scantiest of all in regard to the relations between the Afghans and the Sultan. The only occasion upon which Abdul Hamid is known to have exerted his influence by an official mission to Kabul was at the time of the last Afghan War, when our own relations with Turkey still retained the cordial character they had acquired at the Berlin Congress. The Sultan's influence was then exercised towards the restoration of peace between Afghanistan and India. Shortly afterwards, however, the wind shifted at Yeldiz, and Abdul Hamid sent his former envoy at Kabul to be Turkish Consul-General at Bombay, where the first agency was established for distributing items of news concerning Islam and the Khalif amongst the Mahomedans of the North-West Frontier and Afghanistan. That Afghan Chiefs and Mollahs on their way to and from Mecca are frequent visitors to Yeldiz Kiosk, we know, and some of them are no doubt the bearers of political messages between the Sultan and the Ameer, whilst they all carry back with them to Afghanistan stories, which lose nothing in the telling, of Abdul Hamid's munificence, and of the glories of Islambol—the Persian and Afghan corruption of Stambul—which thus acquires the meaning, " where Islam is plentiful."

It is certainly worth noting that a growing amount of interest has been manifested of late years in the fate of Turkey, and in British policy towards the Sultan, amongst the border tribes of the North-West Frontier, which are in close contact with and to some extent under the influence of the Ameer. It is generally admitted that the excitement and enthusiasm caused by the victories of the Turkish armies over Christian Greece in the spring of 1897 had a good deal to do with the aggressive turbulence of the tribes which led to the Tirah campaign in the autumn of the same year. Last winter I happened to be at Peshawar at the time when the annual jirgahs or meetings between the frontier tribesmen and the British political officers of the frontier take place, and I was struck with the very keen interest which they displayed in our relations with Turkey. The naval demonstration, in which we naturally took a leading part, was being then carried on in connection with the Macedonian question, and the tribesmen made no secret of the disfavour with which they viewed our co-operation in the coercion of Turkey. They had been taught to look upon it solely as an act of hostility towards Islam, and they were not at all inclined to listen to any attempt to discriminate between the Sultan as a temporal ruler and the Khalif as the spiritual head of Islam.

The question of paramount importance to us, however, is whether and to what extent Pan-Islamism has reached the great masses of our Indian Mahomedans, who number roughly one-fifth of the whole population of our Indian Empire, and of whom the vast majority are Sunnis, like the Turks.

It is not infrequently contended that in spite of their large numbers, the Mahomedans of India do not represent a really cohesive force, because they comprise several dissident sects, and consist very largely of the descendants of converts upon whom their religion sits very lightly. There is no doubt some truth in this contention, and to a certain extent Islam may be said never to have entirely prevailed over the more ancient influences of Hinduism. Witness the extent to which caste feeling has preserved its hold upon Indian Mahomedans, though the fundamental conception of caste is absolutely at variance with the democratic principles of the founder of Islam. Again, it may be urged that, as a large number of Indians were won over to Islam by the prospect of relief from the social disabilities imposed upon them by the caste system peculiar to Hinduism, they represent a lower social stratum than the Hindus. This also is true up to a certain point. But on the other hand, it must be remembered that if many of the converts to Islam were drawn from the low caste Hindus, a very considerable number were also drawn from classes influential by their wealth and by their position in every respect except in that of caste. Nor should it be forgotten that amongst the ruling chiefs of India, a good many are themselves Mahomedans, including the most powerful of all, the Nizam of Hyderabad, who rightly prides himself on being the premier-Prince of the Indian Empire. Another argument often used is that after all the Mussulmans only form a majority of the population in a few provinces, such as Eastern Bengal, the Punjab and the North-West Frontier. But against this fact may be set off the other and perhaps more important fact that there is scarcely a single province in which they are not represented, and that their strength lies chiefly in the large towns where public opinion is much more articulate than in the rural districts. They have, above all, and not only in that part of India which was the seat of the Moghul Empire, the prestige which attaches all over the East to a race which has been a ruling race. At various periods during the thousand years which have elapsed since Islam was first imported into India from Arabia and Mesopotamia, Mahomedan dynasties have reigned and flourished in almost every part of the peninsula, and there is scarcely a Hindu whose ancestors have not at one time or another bowed their knee to a Mahomedan ruler. On the whole a careful analysis of the various elements which make up the Mussulman population of India to-day would, I think, show that the Mahomedans occupy a position which cannot be measured merely by their numbers. During the last twenty years there has unquestionably been a growing feeling amongst them all over India that the maintenance of Turkish power and independence is a great Mahomedan interest, in which all Mahomedans are concerned. Amidst the decay of all other Mahomedan States Turkey remains in their eyes the one Power which represents the traditions of militant Islam. As an influential and liberal-minded Mahomedan remarked to me, if Turkey were to disappear, the Mahomedans would become like unto the Jews—a mere religious sect whose kingdom was gone. It is an unfortunate circumstance that the Sultan's policy should have produced so many causes of conflict with England, many of them connected with issues to which the Sultan's emissaries could easily give a sectarian colouring. The public meetings held last year by the Mahomedans in many of the chief Mahomedan centres of India to protest against the coercion of Turkey in connection with Macedonian affairs, were symptomatic of the growth of a feeling which had already become manifest years ago when Lord Salisbury denounced the Sultan himself as the author of the Armenian massacres, and with still less reserve when in the following year Abdul Hamid had once more on European battlefields victoriously wielded "the sword of Islam," though only against so puny a foe as Greece. Even more symptomatic is it that in this very year, just after the acute crisis which nearly ended in open hostilities between Great Britain and Turkey, the Sultan's name-day has been celebrated by the Mahomedans in many parts of India with conspicuous and unexampled fervour. In India, too, as in other parts of the Mahomedan world, the Hejaz Railway has been used by Abdul Hamid as a splendid advertisement for the virtues of Khalifate, and a part of its cost has been defrayed by Indian contributions.

In what light exactly the Mahomedans of India view the Sultan's claim to the Khalifate is a point of no slight interest. In many mosques his name appears to be used in the Friday prayers, but excellent authorities assure us that this does not imply anything more than a mark of respect and reverence for a great Mussulman sovereign. The most interesting pronouncement on this subject is that which was made a few months ago at the time of the Anglo-Turkish differences by Nawab Mohsin-ul-Mulk, the Hon. Secretary of the Mahomedan Anglo-Oriental Club at Aligarh, who has been since the death of Sir Seyyid Ahmad the foremost leader of enlightened Mahomedan opinion. The Nawab gave it as his opinion that if the Indian Moslems speak of the Sultan as Khalif, they do so by way of honouring the greatest Mahomedan king of our time, whose position is rendered still more important by his being servant of the sacred places and the Kaaba. "The term," he added, "is on no account to be taken to mean that Indian Moslems regard him as their ruler in any way, or consider his orders to be binding on them." Quoting from authoritative works on the subject of the rights and duties of the Khalif, the Nawab said it was impossible, having regard to the duties set forth, for any man of even common understanding to think that the Sultan is the Khalif of the Indian Mussulmans in the real sense of the term, or that they are in any matter bound by their religion to obey him. They are the subjects of the King-Emperor, and owe their allegiance to him alone.

It does not, however, follow [he continued] that the Indian Mussulmans have no love for the Sultan of Turkey, or that they do not care for the safety of the Turkish Empire. On the contrary, they all wish with one heart for the stability of Turkish rule, and earnestly pray God that friendly relations between Great Britain and the Porte may be firmly established. Those of us [he said in conclusion] who say they care nothing for the Sultan and for Turkey are either cringing flatterers of the British Government, whom the Government will assuredly never credit, or they have no love for religion. Loyalty towards our Government does not exclude the idea of sympathy with one's co-religionists. Those who think that the two are exclusive of each other are ignorant both of their religious duties and of their political relations.

Another Indian Mahomedan of repute, Hajji Muhammed Ismail Khan, of Dataoli, late member of the Legislative Council of the United Provinces, has recently published a letter on the same subject, and on much the same lines, which, however, contains a noteworthy admission that goes considerably further than the Nawab's letter. For he acknowledges in so many words that "there are certain Mahomedans in India who have a greater love and reverence for the Sultan than is legitimate, or than should really exist. They consider him as a necessary part of their religion." Without wishing to exaggerate the importance of these and other utterances, one cannot but infer from them that the influence which Abdul Hamid is beginning to exercise as the Khalif of Islam over the minds of Indian Mahomedans is causing amongst the more loyal and enlightened section of the Mahomedan community in India a certain measure of apprehension, and that they feel that the time has come openly to discountenance its growth.

This is a matter which deserves very close and serious consideration at the hands of our rulers, especially at a time when the Mahomedans of India are, rightly or wrongly, disposed to believe that their interests no longer receive from the Supreme Government the same impartial treatment to which they had been hitherto accustomed. I do not wish to enter upon controversial questions which have lately been raised in regard to British administration in India, but the fact remains that recent events have produced upon the minds of not a few Indian Mahomedans the impression that their rights as a minority have been sacrificed, and are likely to be still further sacrificed in the future, to the claims of the Hindu majority, and merely, in their opinion, because the Hiudu majority has had recourse to methods of agitation which the Indian Mahomedans have not hitherto considered to be compatible with their deep sense of loyalty towards the British Raj. Their resentment is all the greater in that whatever the antagonism between Christianity and Islam, they have hitherto always believed that there was a certain community of religious thought between Moslems and Christians, which cannot exist between either us or them and the Hindus. We are, like them, as they term it, "*ahl-el-kitab*," people of the Book, that is to say, that we have in common with them a belief in revealed Scriptures, and the Koran to them is only a later revelation which has superseded, but has not destroyed, the sanctity attaching to the Old and New Testament. Above all, they share with us, as they contend, the common ground of a belief in the Unity of God, which should draw us more closely towards them than we can possibly be drawn towards the idolatrous polytheism or pantheism of the Hindus. To these religious considerations are now added political considerations no less weighty, for they rightly contrast the large part which the Mahomedan races of India have borne in the defence of the British Raj with the disloyal agitation of many Hindus, and especially of the noisiest section, the Bengalis, who have, to say the least, never been conspicuous for the martial qualities which the Mahomedans have so often displayed shoulder to shoulder with ourselves. Amongst the younger generation of Mahomedans there is a certain feeling of impatience which cannot be safely ignored. It is finding vent at the present moment in the proposal to establish Mahomedan organisations which shall be as effective for the furtherance of Mahomedan interests as the Indian National Congress is conceived to have been in the furtherance of Hindu interests. Though the Mahomedans may be perfectly sincere at present in protesting that they have no intention of adopting Hindu methods of agitation, one cannot feel quite confident as to what they may do in the future. Should the expectations of the Mahomedans be disappointed, the tendency of these new Mahomedan organisations might well be to seek at least the moral support of their co-religionists beyond the frontier of India, and that is a tendency which Pan-Islamic propagandists would not fail to encourage.

One word in conclusion to deprecate exaggerated apprehensions. It may well be that Pan-Islamism in its present form will not survive the remarkable ruler to whose energy and ability its inception and growth are mainly due. One feature which is in many ways reassuring is that it has achieved greater popularity outside than inside of Turkey proper. None know better than the best class of Turks what Abdul Hamid's policy has cost them, and none deplore more deeply the estrangement of British friendship. So long as Abdul Hamid steers the same course as in the past, all that this country can probably do is to avoid as far as possible any action which can be construed into deliberate hostility to Islam or injustice to our Mahomedan subjects, and especially to our Indian Mahomedans, whose splendid qualities and militant loyalty constitute perhaps the greatest of our Imperial assets in India. But whenever a real change takes place at Constantinople, whether it be in Abdul Hamid's lifetime, or more probably when he is gathered in due course to his forefathers, it may be hoped that whatever British Government is in power will take the earliest opportunity of showing in the face of the Mahomedan world that British policy is inspired by no settled antagonism to Turkey, but on the contrary is prepared to respect and even to support the legitimate exercise of both the temporal and the spiritual authority of the Sultanate, so long as, on the other hand, these are not employed to subserve purposes of hostility to the British Empire.

## DISCUSSION

THE CHAIRMAN: You will agree with me that Mr. Chirol has dealt with this far-reaching subject in what may be regarded as a masterly fashion. To us it is an all-important subject, for as Mr. Chirol has pointed out, the King is ruler over more than half the Mahomedan world, and more than one-fourth of the vast population of India, with its varying religions and races, are Mahomedans. Another point mentioned by Mr. Chirol which I wish to emphasize, is that in the Native Army of India we have a large number of Mahomedans; they form, indeed, a very important part of that bulwark of the British Empire. Of course, as in all religious communities, there is more than one school of thought among our Mahomedan fellow-subjects. There is the old school and the new school—the old school keeping to the traditions of the past with unvarying rigidity, and the new school inclined to the assimilation of Western ideas. But there is one thing on which the Indian Mussulmans as a body are agreed—at least, that is my strong belief. They do not desire that we should transplant Western institutions to India, to an Oriental soil which is not capable of properly fertilizing them. As Mr. Morley remarked in his Budget speech, to think that we can transplant British institutions to a country like India is a ludicrous and fantastic dream. But I do say there are many directions in which we can endeavour to fulfil the loyal and just aspirations of the Indian Mahomedans. They do not yearn for Western institutions, whatever other communities may do, but they do desire to have an adequate share in providing the *personnel* of the administrative machinery of the country. They desire to be adequately represented on such bodies as the district boards, the municipalities, the provincial councils, and the supreme Legislative Council of the Indian Empire. Mr. Chirol has gone over a wide field which it would be impossible for me to attempt to traverse, but I hope we shall have representative points of view brought forward in the discussion.

SIR LEPEL GRIFFIN; As the Chairman has invited me to open the discussion I will not, of course, decline to do so. But I would like to assure Mr. Chirol that his lecture, so far as my view-point is concerned, does away with all possibility of criticism From the first word to the last

I scarcely heard a single sentence with which I am not in full agreement (hear, hear). I think he has put a question of vital moment to our Empire before us very wisely, and, above all, moderately. Moderation is the word which should apply to discussions on such topics more than any other There is no doubt to-day a great revival of Islam in all parts of the world. But if this movement be looked upon with sympathy and generosity by the British Government and the English people, there will be in it no danger to the British Empire. Indeed, I think the tendency will be in the reverse direction. The strong feeling of religious fanaticism (I do not use that word in any harsh manner) always specially pronounced amongst the less civilized people, becomes weaker when spread over a larger civilized area. In all evolution of nations, as well as of other things, you proceed from the simpler to the more complex—from the homogeneous to the heterogeneous. And civilization certainly has this beneficent effect of smoothing asperities and inducing a liberal spirit, the effect which the old tag of our Latin grammars impressed upon us: " Emollit mores nec sinit esse feros."

That is the principal thing I wished to say; but, secondly, I would express my sense of the grave mistake that was made by two great leaders of the English people—Mr. Gladstone and Lord Salisbury—when they, in the most public and emphatic manner, withdrew from Turkey the protection and support of England, declaring that we had put our money on the wrong horse. That was a grave and almost fatal mistake, and the consequences of it have not yet been fully realized. I believe that, seeing how many millions of fellow Mahomedan subjects are included in the Empire, we should frankly recognise the difficulties which beset the Turkish and other Mussulman Governments, and that we should not criticise their methods too harshly, nor interfere too closely with their internal affairs There are many nations in the world whose Governments are not very energetic or very wise, besides those of the Mahomedan States. Let us look more at home, and consider that in our Indian Empire and Army the Mahomedans are the strength of our right arm, and that by our sympathetic attitude we may maintain them in an attitude of warm friendship towards us. It ought not to be forgotten that the progress of Mahomedan learning in all parts of the world during the last thirty years has been most remarkable, and in this is the best and most notable revival of Islam. I see here now three distinguished Mahomedan gentlemen—Mr. Ameer Ali, late Justice of the principal High Court in India; Major Syed Hassan, formerly of the Indian Medical Service, and Mr. Yusuf Ali, one of our Indian Civil Servants, who is just as intelligent and more eloquent than most Englishmen in that Service. In a community which can produce such men there is no lack of ability and no lack of loyalty. I need only add my hearty thanks to Mr. Chirol for his most excellent lecture, which everyone who knows India and the East will thoroughly appreciate and read with interest (cheers).

Mr. AMEER ALI: I have listened with great interest to the admirable lecture which has just been delivered, and with no little admiration for the gift of eloquence by which it was marked. The subject is a very large one, and it is impossible in the time at my disposal to enter into any detailed criticism. Certain remarks, however, suggest themselves to me which may assist the meeting in judging the full significance of the observations which have fallen from the learned lecturer. I may be allowed at the outset to make one personal observation. I do not belong to the Sunni sect, and therefore what I may say as to the claim of the Sultan of Turkey to the Khalifate may at least be regarded as being the opinion of a wholly disinterested person. The lecturer has traversed a very large area, partly historical and partly dealing with the religious and social conditions of Mussulmans in different parts of the world. In his historical survey, the learned lecturer omitted to mention that, whilst the holy cities of Islam and the relics of the Prophet were in the possession of the Khalifs of Baghdad, the Ommeyade sovereigns of Spain never put forward a claim to the title of Khalif. It was only in the ninth century of the Christian era, when Abdul Rahman III came to the throne and found that the Abbaside Khalifs had lost possession of the holy cities, that he assumed the designation of Commander of the Faithful. As regards the title of the Fatimites, most people who have studied Moslem history know how it arose. The lecturer has shown with considerable lucidity, with regard to the claim of the Ottoman sovereigns, how Selim I acquired the title upon the renunciation of the last Khalif of Cairo in his favour. From that time onward the Ottoman claim has been recognised by the bulk of the Sunni world, and most of the ruling Princes and Chiefs of Central and Western Asia. The lecturer is no doubt aware that the Khan of Khiva bears the title, conferred upon the Khans by one of the predecessors of Sultan Abdul Hamid, of Cup Bearer to the Khalif. Other titles, similarly conferred, are borne by other Asiatic rulers. I do not think the learned lecturer is correct, and I say so with all respect, in attributing to the Sultan Abdul Hamid an active part in the propaganda which is supposed by many Westerns to have been set on foot in different parts of the Mahomedan world hostile to non-Moslem forces. If there is any feeling growing in the Mahomedan world in favour of union to assert the rights of Mahomedans against repression or attacks from without, it is due entirely to the extraneous cause of the pressure which is being put upon them by what are called the civilized Powers of Europe in their own interests. It is only natural that the Mahomedans of Algeria, of Morocco, and other parts of Africa, of Arabia, and of Central Asia, should object to be "civilized" at the point of the sword and the bayonet. No one will accuse me of being a reactionary. Those who know me know that my sympathies are entirely on the side of progress and development, and that I am as loyal a subject of Great Britain as any Englishman or Indian can possibly be (cheers). But I cannot overlook the fact that in the name of civilization and Western progress, a great deal has been done which has been most harmful to the healthy development of Mahomedan countries, and which has inspired those Mahomedan nations which still maintain their independence with distrust and distaste for European progress. Look at Bosnia and Herzegovina. The Austrians allege in their favour the construction of roads and hospitals, but of one thing there can be on doubt—in their wake have followed drinking and immorality. The same spectacle presents itself in other parts of the Moslem world brought under European influence. In the eyes of the Mahomedans, civilization coupled with the casino, the *café chantant*, State-recognised immorality, and absinthe drinking does not carry great advantages; and it is very natural in these circumstances that Mahomedan countries should object to the introduction of European authority in their lands. We can perhaps understand their feeling, even though the advocates of civilization may consider it somewhat out of date; but it must not be put down to fanaticism, or to Pan-Islamism, which to certain minds connotes the same idea. The psychology of fanaticism is a complex thing, and must be reserved for discussion on some other occasions. But one observation I must make. Fanaticism may be racial as well as religious. Racial fanaticism is to my mind worse than religious fanaticism, but when the two co-exist, instances of which are abundant, the result is deplorable. Is it not the case that too often when the scions of civilized races leave their homes for other lands, they carry with them a racial fanaticism, which, when superadded to religious fanaticism, sometimes works out in ways that cannot be regarded with satisfaction by enlightened people in the West? So much will perhaps be admitted in favour of Islam that it has no place for racial fanaticism. The Prophet proclaimed from the Mount of Arafat in his last Sermon that all Moslems were brothers. That dictum has never been fully carried into practice by Mahomedans. But I for one should welcome the consummation of Mahomedans in different parts of the world looking upon each other as a brotherhood (hear, hear). Pan-Islamism is a hybrid expression, and I find some difficulty in grasping its meaning. If it means that the Moslems are awakening to that sense of cohesion which has long been in existence in Christendom, then there is no fault to be found with it. But if it is suggested that the word implies a combination of Mahomedans in an aggressive sense—in the sense of hostility to other peoples—then I deny its existence absolutely. I know the Mahomedans of India as well as any man can possibly do; I have my hand upon the pulse of the whole Mahomedan community of Northern India—at any rate, so that I can speak on this matter with some degree of authority. I say that there is no such movement amongst the Mahomedans of India promoted by emissaries of the Sultan, as has been suggested, for the purpose of creating any feeling against the established goverment of the country. I have never come across a single emissary of the Sultan in any part of India. There are a few Turks in Bombay and Calcutta, and occasionally one or two may be found travelling in Northern India; but to regard them as emissaries of the Sultan is a mistake. The Mahomedans of India, as my friend the Nawab Moohsin-ul-Mulk pointed out in the article to which reference has been made, have a natural respect for the greatest Sovereign belonging to their own religion, who holds possession of their most sacred cities, and who is the depositary of the relics of the Prophet. These things, in the eyes of the vast Sunni community, give him the title to be regarded as the inheritor of the Prophet's position, as the spiritual guide of the Sunni world. Beyond that there is no Pan-Islamic movement in India, and to suggest that on account of attachment to the Sultan the Mahomedans there are likely to foster any ill-feeling towards the British Government is an absolute mistake. If the British Government does become unpopular amongst the Mahomedans, it will be the fault of the British Government itself (hear, hear). It will be from want of sympathy with their aspirations. The Mahomedans of India wish to take their rightful place as loyal subjects of the British crown—a loyalty they have displayed in many ways during the last twenty-five years. I may remark in passing that the so-called Wahabi movement in India, to which Mr. Chirol alluded, was a totally different thing to the Wahabi movement in Arabia. It was not Wahabiism but Favaziism. Of course, Mahomedans generally have sympathy with the people of Arabia, the Prophet's own country. They naturally take great interest in the Hedjaz Railway. But anyone looking at the railway without any religious or political prejudice must approve of its construction on humanitarian grounds. Its construction will be of the greatest advantage to pilgrims from all parts of the Moslem world, for it will save them from the delays, privations, and dangers to which they are now exposed in the absence of rapid means of communication between the coast and the holy cities. I cannot believe that British statesmen have such limited conceptions as to think that the railway is intended to be in any way prejudicial to British interests Although not myself acknowledging the spiritual headship of the Sultan of Turkey, I sincerely hope that he will be able to consolidate his power in Arabia, and will use that power in the development of its resources.

I cannot claim to be an admirer of Sultan Abdul Hamid. For one thing, I think he might have given more impetus to the constitutional development of his Empire, and directed more attention to the strengthening of its naval and military resources; that he might have done much more to promote literature and arts. But in keeping in view his failure in these respects we must not lose sight of the difficulties under which he has laboured. For the last two hundred years Turkey has been called upon every quarter of a century to fight for its existence. Can any other nation show the vitality she has exhibited in the face of all her troubles? As Sir Lepel Griffin has shown, it was a mistake which is recognised as such in every part of India for Great Britain to throw over Turkey and leave her to her own resources. If the influence of the British Government in Turkey had been maintained, the course of history in that land would have been very different, and in all probability reform and improvement would have been achieved long ago. (Hear, hear.)

Mr G. de WESSELITSKY: I wish to speak of a revival among my fellow subjects of the Russian Empire who belong to the Mussulman faith. It is a revival, not of Pan-Islamism—I have never seen amongst them, or heard of, a Pan-Islamic propaganda—but a revival of Mussulman feeling, a desire for organization for the advancement of their interests. It is true that in Transcaucasia Tartars were lately in racial feuds with Armenians, from causes which are not clear to me. But with that unfortunate exception the Mahomedans throughout the Russian Empire, whether locally in a minority or in a majority, have shown themselves most law-abiding patient, temperate and industrious, second in all this only to the Russian Old Believers There is a literary Pan-Turkism, an attempt to create a literary language for all the Mussulmans of Russia of Turco-Tartar race common to them with the Turks of the Ottoman Empire, and there is a liberal party amongst them They are taking keen interest in Parliamentary government, and are the first of their co-religionaries in the whole world who are enfranchised and given full political rights. No disabilities are imposed upon the Mahomedans, no difference being made between them and their Christian neighbours. There are many laws made against the Jews, but none against the Mahomedans. There are many Moslem officers and some generals in the Russian army, and also in the civil service. Only recently the Assistant of the Viceroy of the Caucasus, the head of the civil administration there, was a Mussulman. Mussulmans were represented in the first Russian Duma, and they are just now taking part in the elections for the new Duma. I can only say that I hope that my country will persevere in her wise treatment of the Mussulman population I do not speak in any spirit of undue pride. But we in Russia have been so unwise in many other respects that I am desirous of emphasizing the fact that in this respect, at least, our policy has been wise. In the circumstances I have detailed the Mussulmans are good Russian patriots, and there is not the slightest sign in their press or elsewhere that they have been susceptible to any foreign propaganda of the kind spoken of by Mr. Chirol, and here I would like to express my agreement with the most able lecture we have heard. It seems to me that Pan-Islamism might become a very real danger if Mussulmans felt themselves unfairly treated by Christians. But in the measure that Christian Governments treat their Mussulman subjects with justice and grant them equal rights, that danger will disappear, and the Mahomedans will take their place in working for the general good. (Cheers).

Professor T W. ARNOLD: I think that the term "Pan-Islamism" is somewhat of a misnomer; there is really no movement of the kind that has been described to us that embraces the Muhammadan world as a whole. It is important to remember that whole sections of the Muhammadan world are outside the influence of the Ottoman claims Take Morocco, for example; there is no recognition of those claims there, for Morocco has its own Khalifah. Again, there is the case of Persia. No Persian Shiah would ever accept the Sultan as Khalifiah. Though in a minority, the Shiahs of India are a considerable body, and they also would repudiate the Ottoman claims. The Musalmans of China are also to be left out of account in counting the forces of pro-Turkish Pan-Islamism. As to Afghanistan, I have had a great deal to do with Afghan officials, being brought into somewhat intimate intercourse with some of them, and there has never been the slightest indication in their conversation that they accept the claims of Abdul Hamid. And there is a point in this connection with which the lecturer dealt only cursorily—namely, the well-known Hadith, which is accepted as authoritative by all Sunnis, which says that the Khlifah must belong to the tribe of the Quraish. This tradition presents a great difficulty for those journals and speakers in India and elsewhere which uphold the claims of the Sultan of Turkey I remember an occasion, some years ago, when I was sitting with Sir Syed Ahmed, with Nawab Mohsin-ul-Mulk, and with Moulvi Shibli, the secretary of the Nadwat-ul-Ulama, one of the most remarkable movements of our day amongst Muhammadan theologians in India. They were discussing this very question, and they agreed that there was not a single Indian Sunni Maulavi who would dare, as a religious teacher, to say that Indian Muhammadans might reject this tradition. The tradition is found in Al Bukhāri's great collection, and I am told that the Turkish Government refuses to admit into the country any edition of it that includes this obnoxious tradition. The Indian Maulavis say that the movement for recognising the Sultan as Khalifah is largely promoted by journalists who are not theologians This state of affairs is important and noteworthy It means that as soon as in the Sunni community this question of the Khalifate is discussed, there must always arise a theological controversy as to how to dispose of this authoritative tradition There is another consideration. We have in London representatives of most of the Muhammadan populations of the world. There are hundreds of Indians, there are Arabs, there are Persians, there are men from Algiers, from the African East Coast, from South Africa, and from Morocco, We have in London a Pan-Islamic Society which has existed for some years. And what is that Society? I do not know whether even its existence is known in this gathering. It practically consists of one individual. (Laughter.) If there were a real Pan-Islamic movement this Society would have numbers, influence, and power; but it is practically unknown. And even if we accept the claim of the Sultan to be regarded as Khalifah, it is not necessarily a matter to excite alarm, because, as was pointed out by Mr. Ameer Ali, that claim has been recognised in Central Asia for centuries, as is indicated in the titles of the Ameer of Bokhara, the Ameer of Khiva, and other potentates It is not unnatural that the smaller Muhammadan powers should look to the headship of the Sultan, just as the barbarian States looked to Rome, even in the days of her decline, as the head of at least a theoretically united comity. But such sentimental recognition by no means implies any real political relations or united action of any kind. I mention these considerations to show that the Pan-Islamic movement is to some extent a limited one (Hear, hear.)

MAJOR SYED HASSAN, I.M S : The lecturer has placed before you the generally-received view of a movement which it is the fashion to call the "Pan-Islamic" movement or revival. This movement is supposed to be the result of an outburst of fanaticism, inherent in the Mussulman religion and carefully fostered and encouraged by the Sultan of Turkey, with a view to combine all the Mahomedan communities of the world into a formidable opposition to the interests of the great European powers—that in fact the movement is based on religious hatred and directed against Christianity and Christian civilization I am glad the speakers who have preceded me have not subscribed to this doctrine. I ask you to take a much broader view of this question; and with your permission, I will lay before you certain propositions, which I hope to be able to prove on the evidence of well-known and indisputable facts. I do not deny the existence of a movement of some sort, but that movement is not confined to Mussulman countries, and I maintain that it is not a fanatical movement directed against Christianity or the Christian nations, in fact it is not a religious movement at all. Nor is it a racial movement directed against Europeans as such. It has no relation whatever to the religious faith or the nationality of the rulers of a country or to that of its inhabitants. What, then, is the nature of this movement or revival of which we have heard so much of late? Well, we find that there are certain definite and constant conditions under which alone it is found to exist. Where these conditions are absent it cannot live; where they are present it does not fail to flourish. The degree of vitality it acquires and the extent to which it thrives are in direct ratio to the degree of intensity with which the conditions referred to prevail. And these conditions may be summed up in the two words—*Injustice* and *Obscurantism*. Under injustice I include political injustice, judicial injustice (if I may use such an expression) and social injustice—this last referring to all that concerns the personal relations of man to man.

Now, I will illustrate my points by taking first some Mussulman countries. In India there are sixty-two millions of Mahomedans, and yet there the movement known as "Pan-Islamism" is conspicuous by its absence. Why? Because British rule in India, that is to say a Christian rule, is founded on justice. It does care and provide for the intellectual and moral advancement of the people (cheers). It is not absorbed in the mere pursuit of selfish and mercenary aims. Let us take Persia next, and here we find the same movement exacting from a sovereign of the same religious faith and nationality as the people themselves and from an absolute monarch, the rudiments of a constitution, which under favourable circumstances may become the nucleus of a Parliamentary system. In Turkey, again, the so-called "Pan-Islamic" movement is found to exist in an acute form, though not so much on the surface, and is perhaps destined to play an important part in the future development of that unfortunate country. There we find it directed not against Christians, but against the Commander of the Faithful himself and against his régime. In Algeria and in Morocco, specially in the latter, the same movement is directed both against the Mussulman ruler and against the foreign invaders, and for similar reasons.

I will now instance some non-Moslem countries, and we will take China first. Here we find the same phenomenon existing in a Buddhist country, and we might just as well call it "Pan-Buddhism." Here also it has been directed partly against the foreigners, and partly against the effete and antiquated régime of the country itself, and has resulted in a feverish anxiety for reform. Lastly, we will find the same movement actually among the Christian native communities of South Africa, directed against a Christian rule. There it is known as the Ethiopian Church movement, but there is no reason whatsoever why, by analogy it should not be called "Pan-Christianism."

It is evident therefore that the so-called "Pan-Islamic" movement is a universal movement, which has nothing whatsoever to do with religious animosity or bigotry. It is merely a reawakening of the backward races of the world to a sense of their rights and liberties. It is directed against any incubus whatsoever that would suppress or retard as long as possible their moral and intellectual progress. It is, in one word, the revolt of man against *Injustice* and *Obscurantism*. It is aimed against all forms of injustice, under any régime whatsoever, be it native or foreign, Moslem or Christian. The movement is a popular one and is the outcome of the needs and wants actually felt in the present stage of evolution of these backward races—the need for greater liberty, greater activity, more education and greater share in the management of their own affairs.

Now, one word as to the remedy. So far as the European Powers are concerned, the first thing is for them to realize that their economic interests are not so intimately bound up with their political domination as is generally imagined. As a matter of fact, the reverse is often the case. Only one Power seems to have realized this fundamental truth, and that is Germany. Without sacrificing the bones of a single Pomeranian Hussar, she has established for herself an absolutely privileged position in the Moslem world. Her commerce is increasing by leaps and bounds, and she is well on the way to monopolize many markets. More than this, she has come to be looked up to by all Mussulman communities as a sort of protector or patron of their governments and institutions. The lesson for the Powers is, therefore, to make their domination of the backward races as light as circumstances will permit, to avoid all irritating and unnecessary interference with their affairs, and any line of conduct that is likely to be galling to the people or humiliating to their own native rulers. Further, by a course of unswerving justice and attention to the educational requirements of the people, to show them that where they have of necessity to supplant the local despotisms, they substitute something that is worth having, even at the loss of national pride and national independence. If they do all this and base their domination on the goodwill of the people, they will find that their economic interests will thrive to an extent of which they have no conception (cheers).

MR. CHIROL, being called upon to reply, said he would detain them with very few words, and added: I would express a large measure of approval of the interesting remarks of Mr Ameer Ali. I quite think that if we were to talk over the matter we should find that, after all, we were not very far apart in our points of view. The last speaker has covered so very wide a sphere that I am afraid I cannot possibly follow him now. He means, I presume, that there is a very general tendency towards revival, a very general ferment in the Mussulman world, as well as in other great communities all over the world. What I wished to point out was that advantage is being taken of this ferment in the Mussulman world for purposes which, in reality, have nothing to do with the religious merits or, indeed, the ethical merits of the Islamic faith. Movements for reform of the kind Major Syed Hassan has indicated come "from below"; they are popular movements, and are not organized and directed "from above," as is the Pan-Islamic movement, in the form to which I addressed myself (hear, hear).

THE CHAIRMAN: We have listened to an admirable lecture, and we have received a great many valuable observations and much information from the various speakers who have addressed us. Not only because the discussion has been somewhat protracted, but because I think it would be presumptuous to attempt to offer any formal conclusions to you, I shall refrain from putting such opinions as I possess into definite shape at this hour. But there is one point I should like to mention that was brought out by Professor Arnold I have always understood that the fact that the Sultan of Turkey does not belong to the Khoresh tribe is an insuperable bar to his spiritual headship of Islam. However that may be, the subject which Mr. Chirol has dealt with is one of the deepest interest and importance, and what has been said this afternoon will give us cause for reflection. Indeed, to lay down definite conclusions on the somewhat conflicting evidence before us, would require much patient investigation and consideration I will now only ask you to accord to Mr. Chirol a hearty vote of thanks for his able, instructive and informing paper (cheers).

# BIBLIOLIFE

## Old Books Deserve a New Life
www.bibliolife.com

Did you know that you can get most of our titles in our trademark **EasyScript**™ print format? **EasyScript**™ provides readers with a larger than average typeface, for a reading experience that's easier on the eyes.

Did you know that we have an ever-growing collection of books in many languages?

Order online:
www.bibliolife.com/store

Or to exclusively browse our **EasyScript**™ collection:
www.bibliogrande.com

At BiblioLife, we aim to make knowledge more accessible by making thousands of titles available to you – quickly and affordably.

Contact us:
BiblioLife
PO Box 21206
Charleston, SC 29413

Printed in Great Britain by
Amazon.co.uk, Ltd.,
Marston Gate.